IF EVER THERE WAS A REAL-LIFE BRUCE WAYNE, IT'S *MIKHAIL PROKHOROV*. A BILLIONAIRE PLAYBOY WITH A PASSION FOR ATHLETIC ACHIEVEMENT, HE'S THE MOST EXCITING RUSSIAN OF THE 21ST CENTURY. WHETHER RUNNING AN UNLIKELY CAMPAIGN AGAINST VLADIMIR PUTIN OR BUYING HIS WAY INTO THE AMERICAN SPORTS SCENE, PROKHOROV HAS MADE IT IMPOSSIBLE TO IGNORE HIM. HE'S A MAN OF INCREDIBLE AMBITION, AND HE WANTS THE WHOLE WORLD TO KNOW IT.

HIS WEALTH HAS FLUCTUATED CONSIDERABLY IN RECENT YEARS, THANKS TO WILD AMBITIONS, BUT MIKHAIL PROKHOROV HAS BEEN LISTED AS RUSSIA'S *THIRD RICHEST MAN.*

IT'S NOT ONLY HIS WEALTH THAT DISTINGUISHES PROKHOROV. HE'S ALSO *INCREDIBLY TALL,* VIRTUALLY A GIANT AMONG MERE MORTALS, STANDING AT *6'8".*

HE'S GOT AN OUTSIZED REPUTATION, TOO, WITH NICKNAMES SUCH AS *"BACHELOR BILLIONAIRE"* AND *"HOLIDAY MAN"* THAT HE CAN'T SEEM TO SHAKE, NO MATTER WHAT HE ACCOMPLISHES PROFESSIONALLY.

PERSONALLY, HE'S MOST OFTEN DESCRIBED SIMPLY AS A BACHELOR AND MARTIAL ARTS BUFF.

HE IS BEST DESCRIBED, HOWEVER, AS A MAN OF AMBITION. IT DOESN'T ALWAYS WORK OUT, BUT WHAT CAN YOU DO?
HE LOST **5 BILLION** IN TWELVE MONTHS.
BARCLAYS
BARCLAYS CENTER
HE OWNS **45%** OF THE REAL ESTATE PROJECT CURRENTLY DEVELOPING BROOKLYN'S ***ATLANTIC YARDS***, WHERE THE NBA'S ***NETS*** WILL RELOCATE IN SEPTEMBER 2012, PLAYING AT ***BARCLAYS ARENA***.
BARCLAYS
HE ALSO OWNS THE NETS.
HE'S ALSO INVESTED ***200 MILLION*** IN RUSSIA'S FIRST HYBRID CAR, THE ***YO***.

MIKHAIL PROKHOROV WAS BORN ON MAY 5, 1965 IN MOSCOW. BOTH PARENTS UNDERSTOOD THE VALUE OF AMBITION. HIS FATHER HELPED RUN THE *INTERNATIONAL RELATIONS DEPARTMENT* OF THE *SOVIET STATE SPORTS COMMITTEE* WHILE HIS MOTHER DID SCIENTIFIC RESEARCH AT THE *MOSCOW CHEMICAL MATERIALS INSTITUTE*. HIS OLDER SISTER *IRINA* WENT ON TO BECOME AN IMPORTANT MEMBER OF THE RUSSIAN LITERARY SCENE.

PROKHOROV LEARNED ALL ABOUT STRONG WORK ETHICS, A LOVE OF LEARNING, AND SPORTS TRAINING, ALL THINGS THAT WOULD SERVE HIM WELL IN HIS LATER LIFE.

IN SECONDARY EDUCATION, PROKHOROV HAD A FOCUS ON ENGLISH STUDIES, ALREADY BROADENING HIS WORLDVIEW SO HE COULD BETTER UNDERSTAND THE CHALLENGES HE WAS PREPARING TO TACKLE.

HIS STUDIES NEXT TOOK HIM TO THE *MOSCOW FINANCE INSTITUTE* (NOW KNOWN AS THE *FINANCE ACADEMY*), WHERE PROKHOROV STARTED TO MOLD HIS INCREDIBLE MIND FOR BUSINESS.

NOT SURPRISINGLY, HE GRADUATED *MAGNA CUM LAUDE*, IN 1989, FROM THE *INTERNATIONAL ECONOMIC RELATIONS DEPARTMENT.*

WASTING LITTLE TIME, PROKHOROV QUICKLY TRANSITIONED INTO PRACTICAL CONCERNS. HE BECAME HEAD OF THE *MANAGEMENT BOARD DEPARTMENT* AT THE *INTERNATIONAL BANK FOR ECONOMIC COOPERATION* LATER THAT YEAR, A POST HE HELD UNTIL 1992.

HE HAD HIS FIRST TURN AS *CHAIRMAN OF THE BOARD* FOR THE *INTERNATIONAL FINANCE COMPANY* IN 1992, BUT A YEAR LATER TOOK THE SAME POSITION AT *ONEXIM BANK*, WHICH HE HOLDS TO THIS DAY.

HE'S ALSO SERVED AS *PRESIDENT* FOR ONEXIM TWICE, FROM *1998-2000* AND *2007-2011*.

HE WAS PRESIDENT AT *ROSBANK*, TOO, FROM *2000-2001*.

FROM *2001-2007*, PROKHOROV WAS ALSO *GENERAL DIRECTOR* AND *CHAIRMAN OF THE BOARD* FOR *MMC NORILSK NICKEL*.

ARE YOU IMPRESSED YET?

THERE'S MORE!

ANOTHER OF HIS ENDURING BUSINESS ASSOCIATIONS IS WITH *OJSC POLYUS GOLD*, WHERE HE WAS *CHAIRMAN OF THE BOARD* IN 2006.

IN 2004, HE LAUNCHED THE CULTURAL INITIATIVES CHARITABLE FOUNDATION, BUT YOU CAN ALSO CALL IT THE *MIKHAIL PROKHOROV FOUNDATION*.

POLYUS
Chairman of the Board

HE'S BEEN *CEO* THERE, ENDING A SIX MONTH TENURE IN JUNE 2011.

BUT IT'S NOT ALWAYS BUSINESS. I SAID HE WAS A SPORTS ENTHUSIAST, TOO. IN 2008 PROKHOROV BECAME THE HEAD OF THE *RUSSIAN UNION OF BIATHLONISTS*.

PROKHOROV IS A BRILLIANT FINANCIAL MIND, AND HIS GOAL IS NOT JUST TO SEE RUSSIA PROSPER, BUT THE ENTIRE GLOBAL ECONOMY. TO THAT END, ON JULY 2, 1998 HE GAVE HIS *"INNOVATION BREAKTHROUGH"* SPEECH AT THE 4TH ANNUAL **NATIONAL BUSINESS CONFERENCE,** WHERE HE OUTLINED HIS IDEAS FOR THE FUTURE OF BOTH HIS OWN COUNTRY BUT HE IT WOULD BENEFIT EVERYONE. HE SAW THE CHALLENGE AS BROKEN INTO THREE PARTS:

1) BUILDING NATIONAL INNOVATION THROUGH AN INTERNATIONAL PERSPECTIVE.

2) THE USE OF RUSSIAN INTELLECTUALS WHO LIVE IN OTHER COUNTRIES AS VOLUNTARY AMBASSADORS.

3) MODERNIZE COMPETITIVE ADVANTAGES.

BASICALLY, PROKHOROV SEES "INNOVATION BREAKTHROUGH" AS UTILIZING AVAILABLE RESOURCES RATHER THAN RELYING ON OUTDATED STRATEGIES, SOMETHING HE'S DONE THROUGHOUT HIS BUSINESS CAREER.

PROKHOROV DOESN'T BELIEVE IN HIDING HIS OPINIONS. HE BELIEVES, FOR INSTANCE, THAT THE WORLD ECONOMIC CRISIS CAN BEST BE SOLVED BY A NEW FUNDAMENTAL BASIS FOR TRUST.

CARE TO HEAR MORE?

"THE BIGGEST RISK IN BUSINESS AROUND THE WORLD IS THE RISK OF BEING INEFFECTIVE."

"YOU HAVE TO DEVELOP DIVERSE INTERESTS WHICH ARE RELATED TO YOUR OCCUPATION AND HELP ENHANCE YOUR MENTAL CAPACITY, CREATIVITY, AND INTERSYSTEM THINKING."

"PEOPLE ARE NOT ANGRY AT THE RICH. THEY ARE ANGRY AT LYING, CENSORSHIP, AND THE POLICE."

(SOMETIMES IT MAY HELP TO BE RUSSIAN TO UNDERSTAND WHAT HE'S TALKING ABOUT.)

IF I'VE GIVEN YOU THE IMPRESSION THAT IT'S ALWAYS GREAT TO BE MIKHAIL PROKHOROV, NOW'S YOUR CHANCE TO SEE HIM IN A DIFFERENT LIGHT. IN 2007, FOR INSTANCE, HE DEMANDED AN APOLOGY FROM FRANCE AFTER BEING ARRESTED AT A SKI RESORT.

REMEMBER WHEN I SAID PROKHOROV HAD A REPUTATION FOR BEING A PLAYBOY BILLIONAIRE? THAT REPUTATION IS NOT ALWAYS A GOOD THING.

HE LOST *2 MILLION* IN 2008. RELAX, THOUGH. THIS TIME IT WAS A DONATION FOR A RETROSPECTIVE ON THE ART OF *ILYA KABAKOV*.

LATER THAT YEAR, THOUGH, PROKHOROV ENDED HIS LONG-STANDING BUSINESS ASSOCIATION WITH *VLADIMIR POTANIN*. IT WAS NOT AMICABLE.

IN 2009, THE *NEW YORKER* DID A PROFILE ON PROKHOROV, FURTHER PROVING THAT HE HAD BECOME A MAJOR INTERNATIONAL PLAYER.

PRICE $4.50

THE
NEW YORKER
AUG.

Mikhail Prokhorov

profile on Prokhorov, further proving that he had become a major international player

FRANCE DROPPED A PROSTITUTION CASE AGAINST HIM, TOO! (I'LL BET HE LIKED THE PUBLICITY IN THE MAGAZINE BETTER.)

HE BURIED THE HATCHET WITH THE *MOSCOW TIMES* IN THE SAME PERIOD, AFTER SOME UNFLATTERING REMARKS CONCERNING WHAT TRANSPIRED BETWEEN PROKHOROV AND FORMER BUSINESS PARTNER VLADIMIR POTANIN.

The 🛡 Moscow Times

No. 34285   WWW.THEMOSCOWTIMES.COM   JUNE 8 – 11, 2009 WEEKEND

He buried the hatchet

He buried the hatchet with the Moscow Times in the same period, after some unflattering remarks concerning what transpired between Prokhorov and former business partner Vladimir Potanin.

R

Сноб.   Сноб.

Михаил Прохоров

HE LAUNCHED *SNOB* MAGAZINE IN 2010, A RUSSIAN-LANGUAGE PUBLICATION IN THE UNITED STATES. (HE PROBABLY GETS BETTER PRESS IN THESE PAGES.)

BY THE WAY, PROKHOROV ISN'T SHY. HE STATED IN 2010 THAT THE RUSSIAN ELITE HAS BEEN OUT OF TOUCH FOR CENTURIES. (A LITTLE OVER A YEAR LATER, HE WAS RUNNING FOR PRESIDENT.)

IN EARLY 2011, HE CLAIMED THAT THE NETS WOULD WIN A CHAMPIONSHIP WITHIN FOUR SEASONS.

OF COURSE, HE SUFFERED HUMILIATION AT THE *BIATHLON WORLD CUP* SOON AFTER, SO HE CAN PROBABLY APPRECIATE A LITTLE HUMBLE PIE, TOO.

HE REPRESENTED THE SHORT-LIVED *RIGHT CAUSE* POLITICAL PARTY IN 2011, BUT LATER RAN AS AN INDEPENDENT.

PROKHOROV LOVES TO THROW ALL HIS CHIPS ONTO THE TABLE. IN 2012, HE PLEDGED TO DONATE HIS BILLIONS TO CHARITY SHOULD HE PROVE SUCCESSFUL AGAINST *VLADIMIR PUTIN* IN THE RACE FOR THE PRESIDENCY OF RUSSIA.

DONATE
TO
CHARITY

Parties on the French Riviera
Oh, and he's frequently featured in the gossip pages thanks to lavish parties on the French Riviera.

Mikhail Prokhorov

HE LOST A HIGH PROFILE BID FOR *DWIGHT HOWARD* TO JOIN HIS BASKETBALL TEAM. DO EITHER OF THESE THINGS SOUND SUBTLE TO YOU?

OH, AND HE'S FREQUENTLY FEATURED IN THE GOSSIP PAGES THANKS TO LAVISH PARTIES ON THE *FRENCH RIVIERA*.

PROKHOROV HAS EARNED A GREAT DEAL OF RESPECT.

IN 2006 HE WAS AWARDED THE *ORDER OF FRIENDSHIP,* RUSSIAN RECOGNITION FOR HIS CONTRIBUTIONS TO THE COUNTRY'S ECONOMIC POTENTIAL.

besFor

ЕНТ КАПИТАЛИСТА | МАЙ, 2009

100 БОГАТЕЙШИХ БИЗНЕСМЕНОВ

ДОСЬЕ НА КАЖДОГО УЧАСТНИКА РЕЙТИНГА

ПОДСЧЕТ ПОТЕРЬ

HE'S BEEN FEATURED IN *FORBES* MAGAZINE ON THEIR LIST OF BILLIONAIRES, RANKED 54TH IN 2012, WITH A CURRENT WORTH OF *13.2.*

IN 2007, HE WAS APPOINTED TO RUSSIA'S *GOVERNMENT COUNCIL FOR NANOTECHNOLOGY,* WHICH SHOULD HAVE MADE HIS MOTHER PROUD.

NOW ENTERING HIS PRIME, PROKHOROV DECIDED IT WAS TIME TO ENTER POLITICS, WHERE HE COULD BEST LEVERAGE HIS INFLUENCE. HE DECLARED HIS INTENTIONS IN DECEMBER 2011, BUT ANNOUNCED HIS CANDIDACY FOR THE RUSSIAN PRESIDENCY IN JANUARY 2012. FINALLY HE COULD BEGIN TO MAKE HIS LONGSTANDING POLICIES AND OPINIONS A FORCE FOR CHANGE IN HIS COUNTRY, STEPPING OUT OF THE FINANCIAL AND ATHLETIC SPHERES FOR WHICH HE HAD BECOME KNOWN.

THE TRUE COMPLEXITIES OF MODERN RUSSIAN LIFE SOON BECAME APPARENT.

PROKHOROV DISCOVERED THAT HIS IDEALS WERE NOT WHAT BUILT HIS REPUTATION WITH THE GENERAL PUBLIC.

HIS PERSONAL WEALTH MAY HAVE BEEN SEEN AS A DRAWBACK.

MIKHAIL PROKHOROV

THERE MAY HAVE ALSO BEEN THOSE WHO BELIEVED THAT WEALTH HAD BEEN STOLEN FROM THEM, IF NOT BY PROKHOROV DIRECTLY, THEN AT THE VERY LEAST EARNED OFF OF RESOURCES MANIPULATED DURING THE 1990s.

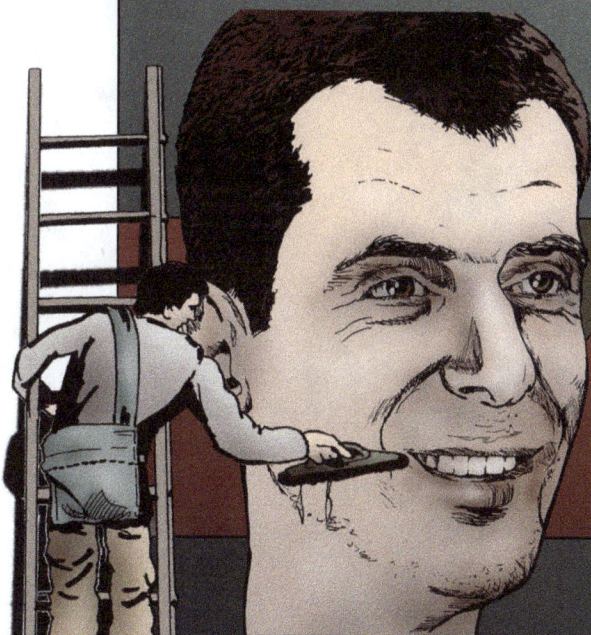

FOR PRESIDENT OF RU...

THERE WERE ALSO SUGGESTIONS THAT PROKHOROV, WORKING FROM A PLATFORM SIMILAR TO THE SENTIMENTS EXPRESSED IN THE UNITED STATES AS *OCCUPY WALL STREET,* WAS IN ACTUALITY A PATSY FOR INCUMBENT PRESIDENT *VLADIMIR PUTIN.*

PROKHOROV ENJOYED SOME UNEXPECTED CELEBRITY DURING THE CAMPAIGN, AND PROBABLY THE BEST PRESS OF HIS CAREER, WITH ONE OF THE MORE UNEXPECTED DECISIONS OF HIS LIFE.

HE STARTED RAPPING, AND CALLED HIMSELF THE *"RUSSIAN EMINEM."* THE PERFORMANCE WAS CALLED BOTH *CHARMING* AND *HORRIBLE*. IT WAS UNIQUE FOR A POLITICIAN IN ANY COUNTRY.

Путин победит
на выборах

STILL, PROKHOROV WENT DOWN WITH DEFEAT COME MARCH 4, 2012, LOSING TO PUTIN BY CONVINCING NUMBERS, EARNING 8% OF THE VOTE VERSUS PUTIN'S 64% AND FELLOW CONTENDER (AND COMMUNIST PARTY MEMBER) *GENNADY ZYUGANOV*, WHO CAPTURED 17%.

TALK OF CORRUPTION IN THE VOTING PROCESS HELPED TO ALLEVIATE SOME OF THE STING, AS DID PROKHOROV'S VOW TO CONTINUE HIS FIGHT FOR A BETTER RUSSIAN FUTURE.

A BILLIONAIRE IN TODAY'S ECONOMY MAY NOT EXPECT TO GARNER TOO MUCH RESPECT FROM THE GENERAL PUBLIC, BUT EVEN SOMEONE WITH A BRASH REPUTATION LIKE MIKHAIL PROKHOROV CAN BE HAPPY WITH WHAT HE'S ACCOMPLISHED WITH HIS GIFTS SO FAR, USING HIS KEEN BUSINESS ACUMEN TO PUSH FOR A MORE PROSPEROUS TOMORROW, NOT JUST FOR HIS FELLOW RUSSIANS, BUT FOR EVERYONE. YOU CAN THINK OF HIM AS THE GUY WHO OWNS THE NETS OR THE RAPPING POLITICIAN IF YOU LIKE, BUT THE FACT IS, YOU'RE THINKING ABOUT HIM, AND THAT'S A START. HE'LL WORK WITH THAT.

BLUEWATER COMICS

Tony Laplume — **Writer**

Miky Ruiz — **Pencils & Inks**

Christian Peña — **Colorist**

David Hopkins — **Letterer**

Miky Ruiz — **Cover**

Darren G. Davis
Publisher

Jason Schultz
Vice President

Jackie Stickley
New Business Development

Jarred Weisfeld
Literary Manager

Kailey Marsh
Entertainment Manager

Maggie Jessup
Publicity

Nikki Borror
Coordinator

Editor: Bea Kimera

Jaymes Reed
Logo Design

Warren Montgomnery
Production

BLUEWATER COMICS

www.bluewaterprod.com

PORTLAND'S

CONCERT

HALL

TOC
CONCERT HALL

THEOLDCHURCH.ORG

www.ingramcontent.com/pod-product-compliance
Lightning Source LLC
Chambersburg PA
CBHW051349290326
41933CB00042B/3350